A Year in C

	J	F	M	A	M	J	J	A	S	O	N	D
1												
2												
3												
4												
5												
6												
7												
8												
9												
10												
11												
12												
13												
14												
15												
16												
17												
18												
19												
20												
21												
22												
23												
24												
25												
26												
27												
28												
29												
30												
31												

□ **IRRITATED, FRUSTRATED, OR ANGRY**

□ **NERVOUS, STRESSED OR ANXIOUS**

□ **ENERGIZED OR EXCITED**

□ **CALM OR RELAXED**

□ **DEPRESSED, SAD OR EMOTIONAL**

□ **ACTIVE, FOCUSED OR MOTIVATED**

□ **HAPPY, POSITIVE OR OPTIMISTIC**

□ **TIRED, RESTLESS OR UNEASY**

Affirmations

DAILY AFFIRMATIONS

IDEAS & PROMPTS

I'm in charge of how I feel today, and I'm choosing to be happy.

I'm brave enough to climb any mountain.

I have the power to change my story.

I've decided that I'm good enough.

No one can make me feel inferior.

My strength is greater than my struggle.

I'll use my failures as a stepping stone.

It's not their job to like me. It's mine.

Success will be my driving force.

The only person who can defeat me, is me.

I dare to be different.

I do not need other people to be happy.

I deserve love, happiness and success.

I am loved and I am wanted.

I will not apologize for being myself.

Positive Thinking

POSITIVE THOUGHTS:
WRITE DOWN YOUR FAVORITE INSPIRATIONAL PHRASE

Do what makes you Happy

AFFIRMATION:

One Day at a Time

JANUARY

S	M	T	W	T	F	S
		1	2	3	4	5
6	7	8	9	10	11	12
13	14	15	16	17	18	19
20	21	22	23	24	25	26
27	28	29	30	31		

NOTES & REMINDERS

One Day at a Time

MONDAY'S **MOOD**

TUESDAY'S **MOOD**

WEDNESDAY'S **MOOD**

THURSDAY'S **MOOD**

One Day at a Time

FRIDAY'S **MOOD**

SATURDAY'S **MOOD**

SUNDAY'S **MOOD**

THOUGHTS & REFLECTIONS ABOUT THE PAST WEEK

My Mood Today

DRAWING THAT DESCRIBES YOUR **FEELINGS**

It's just a bad day, Not a bad life

Positive Thinking

SELF CARE TO DO LIST:

- [ ] _____
- [ ] _____
- [ ] _____
- [ ] _____
- [ ] _____
- [ ] _____
- [ ] _____
- [ ] _____
- [ ] _____
- [ ] _____
- [ ] _____
- [ ] _____
- [ ] _____
- [ ] _____

PHYSICAL NEEDS

EMOTIONAL NEEDS

HOW I FEEL TODAY

I WANT TO WORK ON...

Self Care Checklist

GOALS	M	T	W	T	F	S	S
Got enough rest	◯	◯	◯	◯	◯	◯	◯
Spent time outdoors	◯	◯	◯	◯	◯	◯	◯
Drank enough water	◯	◯	◯	◯	◯	◯	◯
Spent time doing Something that makes me happy.	◯	◯	◯	◯	◯	◯	◯
Went for a walk or exercised.	◯	◯	◯	◯	◯	◯	◯
Spent time with family	◯	◯	◯	◯	◯	◯	◯
Meditated	◯	◯	◯	◯	◯	◯	◯
Connected with friends	◯	◯	◯	◯	◯	◯	◯
_____	◯	◯	◯	◯	◯	◯	◯
_____	◯	◯	◯	◯	◯	◯	◯
_____	◯	◯	◯	◯	◯	◯	◯

NOTES:

Mood Meter

MONDAY

AM | PM

TUESDAY

AM | PM

SUNDAY

AM | PM

TRACK YOUR MOODS

WEDNESDAY

AM | PM

SATURDAY

AM | PM

FRIDAY

AM | PM

THURSDAY

AM | PM

COLOR SCALE

Grateful Thoughts

THIS WEEK I AM GRATEFUL FOR

I AM BLESSED TO HAVE THESE PEOPLE IN MY LIFE

5 REASONS TO BE THANKFUL

1
2
3
4
5

Me Time

Write down the things that make you happy. Then, check the box every day that you spend time with that activity.

☐	☐	☐	☐	☐	☐	☐

☐	☐	☐	☐	☐	☐	☐

NOTES:

Self Care

DAILY **INSPIRATION**

WATER INTAKE:

FITNESS **GOALS**

One day at a time...

THANKFUL **FOR**

DAILY **MEALS**

BREAKFAST:

_____
_____
_____

LUNCH:

_____
_____

DINNER:

_____
_____

SNACKS:

_____
_____
_____
_____

Personal Goals

MY SELF GOALS FOR THIS YEAR:

2 THINGS I CAN CHANGE TO MEET MY GOALS:

MY GREATEST OBSTACLE GOING FORWARD:

Good things take time

Mental Health Monitor

DAILY

_____
_____
_____
_____
_____
_____
_____
_____
_____
_____
_____

WEEKLY

_____
_____
_____
_____
_____
_____
_____
_____
_____
_____

PERSONAL REFLECTIONS

Self Care Goals

TIME FRAME	MY GOALS	STEPS I'LL TAKE

be wild ~ *be true* ~ *be happy*

Self Care Techniques

MIND

_____
_____
_____
_____
_____
_____
_____
_____
_____
_____

BODY

_____
_____
_____
_____
_____
_____
_____
_____
_____
_____

PERSONAL REFLECTIONS

One Day at a Time

FEBRUARY

S	M	T	W	T	F	S
					1	2
3	4	5	6	7	8	9
10	11	12	13	14	15	16
17	18	19	20	21	22	23
24	25	26	27	28		

NOTES & REMINDERS

One Day at a Time

MONDAY'S **MOOD**

TUESDAY'S **MOOD**

WEDNESDAY'S **MOOD**

THURSDAY'S **MOOD**

One Day at a Time

FRIDAY'S **MOOD**

SATURDAY'S **MOOD**

SUNDAY'S **MOOD**

THOUGHTS & REFLECTIONS ABOUT THE PAST WEEK

Positive Thinking

SELF CARE TO DO LIST:

- [ ] _____
- [ ] _____
- [ ] _____
- [ ] _____
- [ ] _____
- [ ] _____
- [ ] _____
- [ ] _____
- [ ] _____
- [ ] _____
- [ ] _____
- [ ] _____
- [ ] _____
- [ ] _____

PHYSICAL NEEDS

EMOTIONAL NEEDS

HOW I FEEL TODAY

I WANT TO WORK ON...

Mood Meter

COLOR SCALE

Grateful Thoughts

THIS WEEK I AM GRATEFUL FOR

I AM BLESSED TO HAVE THESE PEOPLE IN MY LIFE

5 REASONS TO BE THANKFUL

1
2
3
4
5

Self Care Log

HOW I CAN **MINIMIZE THE NEGATIVITY** IN MY LIFE

POSITIVE STEPS I CAN TAKE TO BE HAPPY

IT ALWAYS SEEMS Impossible UNTIL IT'S DONE

Self Care

DAILY **INSPIRATION**

WATER INTAKE:

FITNESS **GOALS**

_____
_____
_____

One day at a time...

THANKFUL **FOR**

DAILY **MEALS**

BREAKFAST:

_____
_____
_____

LUNCH:

_____
_____

DINNER:

_____
_____

SNACKS:

_____
_____
_____
_____

Personal Goals

MY SELF GOALS FOR THIS YEAR:

2 THINGS I CAN CHANGE TO MEET MY GOALS:

MY GREATEST OBSTACLE GOING FORWARD:

Good things take time

Mental Health Monitor

DAILY

_____

_____

_____

_____

_____

_____

_____

_____

_____

_____

_____

WEEKLY

_____

_____

_____

_____

_____

_____

_____

_____

_____

_____

PERSONAL REFLECTIONS

Self Care Goals

TIME FRAME	MY GOALS	STEPS I'LL TAKE

be wild ~ be true ~ be happy

One Day at a Time

MARCH

S	M	T	W	T	F	S
					1	2
3	4	5	6	7	8	9
10	11	12	13	14	15	16
17	18	19	20	21	22	23
24	25	26	27	28	29	30
31						

NOTES & REMINDERS

One Day at a Time

MONDAY'S **MOOD**

TUESDAY'S **MOOD**

WEDNESDAY'S **MOOD**

THURSDAY'S **MOOD**

One Day at a Time

FRIDAY'S **MOOD**

SATURDAY'S **MOOD**

SUNDAY'S **MOOD**

THOUGHTS & REFLECTIONS ABOUT THE PAST WEEK

Positive Thinking

SELF CARE TO DO LIST:

- [ ] _____
- [ ] _____
- [ ] _____
- [ ] _____
- [ ] _____
- [ ] _____
- [ ] _____
- [ ] _____
- [ ] _____
- [ ] _____
- [ ] _____
- [ ] _____
- [ ] _____
- [ ] _____

PHYSICAL NEEDS

EMOTIONAL NEEDS

HOW I FEEL TODAY

I WANT TO WORK ON...

Mood Meter

MONDAY

AM | PM

TUESDAY

AM | PM

SUNDAY

AM | PM

WEDNESDAY

AM | PM

SATURDAY

AM | PM

TRACK YOUR MOODS

FRIDAY

AM | PM

THURSDAY

AM | PM

COLOR SCALE

Grateful Thoughts

THIS WEEK I AM GRATEFUL FOR

I AM BLESSED TO HAVE THESE PEOPLE IN MY LIFE

5 REASONS TO BE THANKFUL

1
2
3
4
5

Self Care Log

HOW I CAN **MINIMIZE THE NEGATIVITY** IN MY LIFE

POSITIVE STEPS I CAN TAKE TO BE HAPPY

Me Time

Write down the things that make you happy. Then, check the box every day that you spend time with that activity.

	☐ ☐ ☐ ☐ ☐ ☐ ☐
	☐ ☐ ☐ ☐ ☐ ☐ ☐
	☐ ☐ ☐ ☐ ☐ ☐ ☐
	☐ ☐ ☐ ☐ ☐ ☐ ☐
	☐ ☐ ☐ ☐ ☐ ☐ ☐
	☐ ☐ ☐ ☐ ☐ ☐ ☐
	☐ ☐ ☐ ☐ ☐ ☐ ☐
	☐ ☐ ☐ ☐ ☐ ☐ ☐

NOTES:

Self Care

DAILY **INSPIRATION**

WATER INTAKE:

FITNESS **GOALS**

_____

_____

_____

One day at a time...

THANKFUL **FOR**

DAILY **MEALS**

BREAKFAST:

_____

_____

_____

LUNCH:

_____

_____

DINNER:

_____

_____

SNACKS:

_____

_____

_____

_____

Personal Goals

MY SELF GOALS FOR THIS YEAR:

2 THINGS I CAN CHANGE TO MEET MY GOALS:

MY GREATEST OBSTACLE GOING FORWARD:

Good things take time

Mental Health Monitor

DAILY

_____

_____

_____

_____

_____

_____

_____

_____

_____

_____

_____

_____

WEEKLY

_____

_____

_____

_____

_____

_____

_____

_____

_____

_____

_____

PERSONAL REFLECTIONS

Self Care Goals

TIME FRAME	MY GOALS	STEPS I'LL TAKE

be wild ~ be true ~ be happy

Self Care Techniques

MIND

_____
_____
_____
_____
_____
_____
_____
_____
_____
_____
_____

BODY

_____
_____
_____
_____
_____
_____
_____
_____
_____
_____
_____

PERSONAL REFLECTIONS

One Day at a Time

APRIL

S	M	T	W	T	F	S
	1	2	3	4	5	6
7	8	9	10	11	12	13
14	15	16	17	18	19	20
21	22	23	24	25	26	27
28	29	30				

NOTES & REMINDERS

One Day at a Time

MONDAY'S **MOOD**

TUESDAY'S **MOOD**

WEDNESDAY'S **MOOD**

THURSDAY'S **MOOD**

One Day at a Time

FRIDAY'S **MOOD**

SATURDAY'S **MOOD**

SUNDAY'S **MOOD**

THOUGHTS & REFLECTIONS ABOUT THE PAST WEEK

Mood Meter

MONDAY

AM | PM

TUESDAY

AM | PM

WEDNESDAY

AM | PM

THURSDAY

PM | AM

FRIDAY

PM | AM

SATURDAY

AM | PM

SUNDAY

AM | PM

TRACK YOUR MOODS

COLOR SCALE

Grateful Thoughts

THIS WEEK I AM GRATEFUL FOR

I AM BLESSED TO HAVE THESE PEOPLE IN MY LIFE

5 REASONS TO BE THANKFUL

1
2
3
4
5

Self Care Log

HOW I CAN **MINIMIZE THE NEGATIVITY** IN MY LIFE

POSITIVE STEPS I CAN TAKE TO BE HAPPY

IT Always SEEMS Impossible UNTIL IT'S DONE

Self Care

DAILY **INSPIRATION**

WATER INTAKE:

FITNESS **GOALS**

_____

_____

_____

One day at a time...

THANKFUL **FOR**

DAILY **MEALS**

BREAKFAST:

_____

_____

_____

LUNCH:

_____

_____

DINNER:

_____

_____

_____

SNACKS:

_____

_____

_____

_____

_____

Personal Goals

MY SELF GOALS FOR THIS YEAR:

2 THINGS I CAN CHANGE TO MEET MY GOALS:

MY GREATEST OBSTACLE GOING FORWARD:

Good things take time

Mental Health Monitor

DAILY

_____
_____
_____
_____
_____
_____
_____
_____
_____
_____
_____
_____

WEEKLY

_____
_____
_____
_____
_____
_____
_____
_____
_____
_____
_____
_____

PERSONAL REFLECTIONS

Self Care Goals

TIME FRAME	MY GOALS	STEPS I'LL TAKE

be wild ~ be true ~ be happy

Self Care Techniques

MIND

_____
_____
_____
_____
_____
_____
_____
_____
_____
_____
_____

BODY

_____
_____
_____
_____
_____
_____
_____
_____
_____
_____
_____

PERSONAL REFLECTIONS

One Day at a Time

MAY

S	M	T	W	T	F	S
			1	2	3	4
5	6	7	8	9	10	11
12	13	14	15	16	17	18
19	20	21	22	23	24	25
26	27	28	29	30	31	

NOTES & REMINDERS

One Day at a Time

MONDAY'S **MOOD**

TUESDAY'S **MOOD**

WEDNESDAY'S **MOOD**

THURSDAY'S **MOOD**

One Day at a Time

FRIDAY'S **MOOD**

SATURDAY'S **MOOD**

SUNDAY'S **MOOD**

THOUGHTS & REFLECTIONS ABOUT THE PAST WEEK

My Mood Today

DRAWING THAT DESCRIBES YOUR **FEELINGS**

It's just a bad day, Not a bad life

Positive Thinking

SELF CARE TO DO LIST:

- [ ] _____
- [ ] _____
- [ ] _____
- [ ] _____
- [ ] _____
- [ ] _____
- [ ] _____
- [ ] _____
- [ ] _____
- [ ] _____
- [ ] _____
- [ ] _____
- [ ] _____
- [ ] _____

PHYSICAL NEEDS

EMOTIONAL NEEDS

HOW I FEEL TODAY

I WANT TO WORK ON...

Mood Meter

MONDAY

AM PM

TUESDAY

AM PM

SUNDAY

AM PM

TRACK YOUR MOODS

WEDNESDAY

AM PM

SATURDAY

AM PM

FRIDAY

AM PM

THURSDAY

PM AM

COLOR SCALE

Grateful Thoughts

THIS WEEK I AM GRATEFUL FOR

I AM BLESSED TO HAVE THESE PEOPLE IN MY LIFE

5 REASONS TO BE THANKFUL

1
2
3
4
5

Self Care Log

HOW I CAN **MINIMIZE THE NEGATIVITY** IN MY LIFE

POSITIVE STEPS I CAN TAKE TO BE HAPPY

IT ALWAYS SEEMS Impossible UNTIL IT'S DONE

Me Time

Write down the things that make you happy. Then, check the box every day that you spend time with that activity.

☐	☐	☐	☐	☐	☐	☐

☐	☐	☐	☐	☐	☐	☐

☐	☐	☐	☐	☐	☐	☐

☐	☐	☐	☐	☐	☐	☐

☐	☐	☐	☐	☐	☐	☐

☐	☐	☐	☐	☐	☐	☐

☐	☐	☐	☐	☐	☐	☐

☐	☐	☐	☐	☐	☐	☐

NOTES:

Self Care

DAILY **INSPIRATION**

DAILY **MEALS**

BREAKFAST:

_____

_____

_____

LUNCH:

_____

_____

WATER INTAKE:

FITNESS **GOALS**

_____

_____

_____

DINNER:

_____

_____

_____

One day at a time...

THANKFUL **FOR**

SNACKS:

_____

_____

_____

_____

_____

Personal Goals

MY SELF GOALS FOR THIS YEAR:

2 THINGS I CAN CHANGE TO MEET MY GOALS:

MY GREATEST OBSTACLE GOING FORWARD:

Good things take time

Mental Health Monitor

DAILY

_____
_____
_____
_____
_____
_____
_____
_____
_____
_____

WEEKLY

_____
_____
_____
_____
_____
_____
_____
_____
_____
_____

PERSONAL REFLECTIONS

Self Care Goals

TIME FRAME	MY GOALS	STEPS I'LL TAKE

be wild ~ be true ~ be happy

Self Care Techniques

MIND

_____
_____
_____
_____
_____
_____
_____
_____
_____
_____
_____
_____

BODY

_____
_____
_____
_____
_____
_____
_____
_____
_____
_____
_____
_____

PERSONAL REFLECTIONS

One Day at a Time

JUNE						
S	M	T	W	T	F	S
						1
2	3	4	5	6	7	8
9	10	11	12	13	14	15
16	17	18	19	20	21	22
23	24	25	26	27	28	29
30						

NOTES & REMINDERS

One Day at a Time

MONDAY'S **MOOD**

TUESDAY'S **MOOD**

WEDNESDAY'S **MOOD**

Good things take time

THURSDAY'S **MOOD**

One Day at a Time

FRIDAY'S **MOOD**

SATURDAY'S **MOOD**

SUNDAY'S **MOOD**

THOUGHTS & REFLECTIONS ABOUT THE PAST WEEK

Positive Thinking

SELF CARE TO DO LIST:

- ☐ _____
- ☐ _____
- ☐ _____
- ☐ _____
- ☐ _____
- ☐ _____
- ☐ _____
- ☐ _____
- ☐ _____
- ☐ _____
- ☐ _____
- ☐ _____
- ☐ _____
- ☐

PHYSICAL NEEDS

EMOTIONAL NEEDS

HOW I FEEL TODAY

I WANT TO WORK ON...

Mood Meter

MONDAY
AM | PM

TUESDAY
AM | PM

WEDNESDAY
AM | PM

THURSDAY
AM | PM

FRIDAY
AM | PM

SATURDAY
AM | PM

SUNDAY
AM | PM

TRACK YOUR MOODS

COLOR SCALE

Grateful Thoughts

THIS WEEK I AM GRATEFUL FOR

I AM BLESSED TO HAVE THESE PEOPLE IN MY LIFE

5 REASONS TO BE THANKFUL

1
2
3
4
5

Self Care Log

HOW I CAN **MINIMIZE THE NEGATIVITY** IN MY LIFE

POSITIVE STEPS I CAN TAKE TO BE HAPPY

Me Time

Write down the things that make you happy. Then, check the box every day that you spend time with that activity.

	☐	☐	☐	☐	☐	☐	☐
	☐	☐	☐	☐	☐	☐	☐
	☐	☐	☐	☐	☐	☐	☐
	☐	☐	☐	☐	☐	☐	☐
	☐	☐	☐	☐	☐	☐	☐
	☐	☐	☐	☐	☐	☐	☐
	☐	☐	☐	☐	☐	☐	☐
	☐	☐	☐	☐	☐	☐	☐

NOTES:

Self Care

DAILY **INSPIRATION**

DAILY **MEALS**

BREAKFAST:

_____

_____

_____

LUNCH:

_____

_____

WATER INTAKE:

FITNESS **GOALS**

_____

_____

_____

DINNER:

_____

_____

_____

One day at a time...

SNACKS:

THANKFUL **FOR**

_____

_____

_____

_____

_____

_____

Personal Goals

MY SELF GOALS FOR THIS YEAR:

2 THINGS I CAN CHANGE TO MEET MY GOALS:

MY GREATEST OBSTACLE GOING FORWARD:

Good things take time

Mental Health Monitor

DAILY

_____

_____

_____

_____

_____

_____

_____

_____

_____

_____

_____

WEEKLY

_____

_____

_____

_____

_____

_____

_____

_____

_____

_____

_____

PERSONAL REFLECTIONS

Self Care Goals

TIME FRAME	MY GOALS	STEPS I'LL TAKE

be wild ～ be true ～ be happy

Self Care Techniques

MIND

_____
_____
_____
_____
_____
_____
_____
_____
_____
_____
_____

BODY

_____
_____
_____
_____
_____
_____
_____
_____
_____
_____
_____

PERSONAL REFLECTIONS

One Day at a Time

JULY

S	M	T	W	T	F	S
	1	2	3	4	5	6
7	8	9	10	11	12	13
14	15	16	17	18	19	20
21	22	23	24	25	26	27
28	29	30	31			

NOTES & REMINDERS

One Day at a Time

MONDAY'S **MOOD**

TUESDAY'S **MOOD**

WEDNESDAY'S **MOOD**

THURSDAY'S **MOOD**

One Day at a Time

FRIDAY'S **MOOD**

SATURDAY'S **MOOD**

SUNDAY'S **MOOD**

THOUGHTS & REFLECTIONS ABOUT THE PAST WEEK

Positive Thinking

SELF CARE TO DO LIST:

- [ ] _____
- [ ] _____
- [ ] _____
- [ ] _____
- [ ] _____
- [ ] _____
- [ ] _____
- [ ] _____
- [ ] _____
- [ ] _____
- [ ] _____
- [ ] _____
- [ ] _____
- [ ] _____

PHYSICAL NEEDS

EMOTIONAL NEEDS

HOW I FEEL TODAY

I WANT TO WORK ON...

Mood Meter

TRACK YOUR MOODS

MONDAY
AM | PM

TUESDAY
AM | PM

WEDNESDAY
AM | PM

THURSDAY
PM | AM

FRIDAY
PM | AM

SATURDAY
AM | PM

SUNDAY
AM | PM

COLOR SCALE

Grateful Thoughts

THIS WEEK I AM GRATEFUL FOR

I AM BLESSED TO HAVE THESE PEOPLE IN MY LIFE

5 REASONS TO BE THANKFUL

1
2
3
4
5

Self Care Log

HOW I CAN **MINIMIZE THE NEGATIVITY** IN MY LIFE

POSITIVE STEPS I CAN TAKE TO BE HAPPY

IT Always SEEMS Impossible UNTIL IT'S DONE

Me Time

Write down the things that make you happy. Then, check the box every day that you spend time with that activity.

	☐	☐	☐	☐	☐	☐
	☐	☐	☐	☐	☐	☐
	☐	☐	☐	☐	☐	☐
	☐	☐	☐	☐	☐	☐
	☐	☐	☐	☐	☐	☐
	☐	☐	☐	☐	☐	☐
	☐	☐	☐	☐	☐	☐
	☐	☐	☐	☐	☐	☐

NOTES:

Self Care

DAILY **INSPIRATION**

WATER INTAKE:

FITNESS **GOALS**

_____
_____
_____

One day at a time...

THANKFUL **FOR**

DAILY **MEALS**

BREAKFAST:

_____
_____
_____

LUNCH:

_____
_____

DINNER:

_____
_____
_____

SNACKS:

_____
_____
_____
_____

Personal Goals

MY SELF GOALS FOR THIS YEAR:

2 THINGS I CAN CHANGE TO MEET MY GOALS:

MY GREATEST OBSTACLE GOING FORWARD:

Good things take time

Mental Health Monitor

DAILY

_____
_____
_____
_____
_____
_____
_____
_____
_____
_____
_____

WEEKLY

_____
_____
_____
_____
_____
_____
_____
_____
_____
_____
_____

PERSONAL REFLECTIONS

Self Care Goals

TIME FRAME	MY GOALS	STEPS I'LL TAKE

be wild ~ be true ~ be happy

Self Care Techniques

MIND

_____
_____
_____
_____
_____
_____
_____
_____
_____
_____
_____

BODY

_____
_____
_____
_____
_____
_____
_____
_____
_____
_____
_____

PERSONAL REFLECTIONS

One Day at a Time

AUGUST

S	M	T	W	T	F	S
				1	2	3
4	5	6	7	8	9	10
11	12	13	14	15	16	17
18	19	20	21	22	23	24
25	26	27	28	29	30	31

NOTES & REMINDERS

One Day at a Time

MONDAY'S **MOOD**

TUESDAY'S **MOOD**

WEDNESDAY'S **MOOD**

THURSDAY'S **MOOD**

One Day at a Time

FRIDAY'S **MOOD**

SATURDAY'S **MOOD**

SUNDAY'S **MOOD**

THOUGHTS & REFLECTIONS ABOUT THE PAST WEEK

Positive Thinking

SELF CARE TO DO LIST:

- ☐ _____
- ☐ _____
- ☐ _____
- ☐ _____
- ☐ _____
- ☐ _____
- ☐ _____
- ☐ _____
- ☐ _____
- ☐ _____
- ☐ _____
- ☐ _____
- ☐ _____
- ☐ _____

PHYSICAL NEEDS

EMOTIONAL NEEDS

HOW I FEEL TODAY

I WANT TO WORK ON...

Mood Meter

MONDAY

TUESDAY

WEDNESDAY

THURSDAY

FRIDAY

SATURDAY

SUNDAY

TRACK YOUR MOODS

COLOR SCALE

Grateful Thoughts

THIS WEEK I AM GRATEFUL FOR

I AM BLESSED TO HAVE THESE PEOPLE IN MY LIFE

5 REASONS TO BE THANKFUL

1
2
3
4
5

Self Care Log

HOW I CAN **MINIMIZE THE NEGATIVITY** IN MY LIFE

POSITIVE STEPS I CAN TAKE TO BE HAPPY

IT ALWAYS SEEMS Impossible UNTIL IT'S DONE

Me Time

Write down the things that make you happy. Then, check the box every day that you spend time with that activity.

	☐	☐	☐	☐	☐	☐	☐
	☐	☐	☐	☐	☐	☐	☐
	☐	☐	☐	☐	☐	☐	☐
	☐	☐	☐	☐	☐	☐	☐
	☐	☐	☐	☐	☐	☐	☐
	☐	☐	☐	☐	☐	☐	☐
	☐	☐	☐	☐	☐	☐	☐
	☐	☐	☐	☐	☐	☐	☐

NOTES:

Self Care

DAILY **INSPIRATION**

DAILY **MEALS**

BREAKFAST:

_____
_____
_____

LUNCH:

_____
_____
_____

DINNER:

_____
_____
_____

SNACKS:

_____
_____
_____
_____
_____

WATER INTAKE:

FITNESS **GOALS**

_____
_____
_____

One day at a time...

THANKFUL **FOR**

Personal Goals

MY SELF GOALS FOR THIS YEAR:

2 THINGS I CAN CHANGE TO MEET MY GOALS:

MY GREATEST OBSTACLE GOING FORWARD:

Good things take time

Mental Health Monitor

DAILY

_____
_____
_____
_____
_____
_____
_____
_____
_____
_____
_____
_____

WEEKLY

_____
_____
_____
_____
_____
_____
_____
_____
_____
_____
_____
_____

PERSONAL REFLECTIONS

Self Care Goals

TIME FRAME	MY GOALS	STEPS I'LL TAKE

be wild ~ be true ~ be happy

Self Care Techniques

MIND

_____
_____
_____
_____
_____
_____
_____
_____
_____
_____
_____

BODY

_____
_____
_____
_____
_____
_____
_____
_____
_____
_____
_____

PERSONAL REFLECTIONS

One Day at a Time

SEPTEMBER

S	M	T	W	T	F	S
1	2	3	4	5	6	7
8	9	10	11	12	13	14
15	16	17	18	19	20	21
22	23	24	25	26	27	28
29	30					

NOTES & REMINDERS

One Day at a Time

MONDAY'S **MOOD**

TUESDAY'S **MOOD**

WEDNESDAY'S **MOOD**

THURSDAY'S **MOOD**

One Day at a Time

FRIDAY'S **MOOD**

SATURDAY'S **MOOD**

SUNDAY'S **MOOD**

THOUGHTS & REFLECTIONS ABOUT THE PAST WEEK

Positive Thinking

SELF CARE TO DO LIST:

- [ ] _____
- [ ] _____
- [ ] _____
- [ ] _____
- [ ] _____
- [ ] _____
- [ ] _____
- [ ] _____
- [ ] _____
- [ ] _____
- [ ] _____
- [ ] _____
- [ ] _____
- [ ] _____

PHYSICAL NEEDS

EMOTIONAL NEEDS

HOW I FEEL TODAY

I WANT TO WORK ON...

Mood Meter

MONDAY

AM | PM

TUESDAY

AM | PM

SUNDAY

AM | PM

TRACK YOUR MOODS

WEDNESDAY

AM | PM

SATURDAY

AM | PM

FRIDAY

PM | AM

THURSDAY

AM | PM

COLOR SCALE

Grateful Thoughts

THIS WEEK I AM GRATEFUL FOR

I AM BLESSED TO HAVE THESE PEOPLE IN MY LIFE

5 REASONS TO BE THANKFUL

1
2
3
4
5

Self Care Log

HOW I CAN **MINIMIZE THE NEGATIVITY** IN MY LIFE

POSITIVE STEPS I CAN TAKE TO BE HAPPY

Me Time

Write down the things that make you happy. Then, check the box every day that you spend time with that activity.

☐	☐	☐	☐	☐	☐	☐

☐	☐	☐	☐	☐	☐	☐

☐	☐	☐	☐	☐	☐	☐

☐	☐	☐	☐	☐	☐	☐

☐	☐	☐	☐	☐	☐	☐

☐	☐	☐	☐	☐	☐	☐

☐	☐	☐	☐	☐	☐	☐

☐	☐	☐	☐	☐	☐	☐

NOTES:

Self Care

DAILY **INSPIRATION**

WATER INTAKE:

FITNESS **GOALS**

_____

_____

_____

One day at a time...

THANKFUL **FOR**

DAILY **MEALS**

BREAKFAST:

_____

_____

LUNCH:

_____

_____

DINNER:

_____

_____

SNACKS:

_____

_____

_____

_____

Personal Goals

MY SELF GOALS FOR THIS YEAR:

2 THINGS I CAN CHANGE TO MEET MY GOALS:

MY GREATEST OBSTACLE GOING FORWARD:

Good things take time

Mental Health Monitor

DAILY

_____
_____
_____
_____
_____
_____
_____
_____
_____
_____
_____
_____

WEEKLY

_____
_____
_____
_____
_____
_____
_____
_____
_____
_____
_____

PERSONAL REFLECTIONS

Self Care Goals

TIME FRAME	MY GOALS	STEPS I'LL TAKE

be wild ~ be true ~ be happy

Self Care Techniques

MIND

_____
_____
_____
_____
_____
_____
_____
_____
_____
_____
_____

BODY

_____
_____
_____
_____
_____
_____
_____
_____
_____
_____
_____

PERSONAL REFLECTIONS

One Day at a Time

OCTOBER

S	M	T	W	T	F	S
		1	2	3	4	5
6	7	8	9	10	11	12
13	14	15	16	17	18	19
20	21	22	23	24	25	26
27	28	29	30	31		

NOTES & REMINDERS

One Day at a Time

MONDAY'S **MOOD**

TUESDAY'S **MOOD**

WEDNESDAY'S **MOOD**

THURSDAY'S **MOOD**

One Day at a Time

FRIDAY'S **MOOD**

SATURDAY'S **MOOD**

SUNDAY'S **MOOD**

THOUGHTS & REFLECTIONS ABOUT THE PAST WEEK

Positive Thinking

SELF CARE TO DO LIST:

- [ ] _____
- [ ] _____
- [ ] _____
- [ ] _____
- [ ] _____
- [ ] _____
- [ ] _____
- [ ] _____
- [ ] _____
- [ ] _____
- [ ] _____
- [ ] _____
- [ ] _____
- [ ] _____

PHYSICAL NEEDS

EMOTIONAL NEEDS

HOW I FEEL TODAY

I WANT TO WORK ON...

Mood Meter

MONDAY

AM | PM

TUESDAY

AM | PM

SUNDAY

AM | PM

TRACK YOUR MOODS

WEDNESDAY

AM | PM

SATURDAY

PM | AM

FRIDAY

PM | AM

THURSDAY

PM | AM

COLOR SCALE

Grateful Thoughts

THIS WEEK I AM GRATEFUL FOR

I AM BLESSED TO HAVE THESE PEOPLE IN MY LIFE

5 REASONS TO BE THANKFUL

1
2
3
4
5

Self Care Log

HOW I CAN **MINIMIZE THE NEGATIVITY** IN MY LIFE

POSITIVE STEPS I CAN TAKE TO BE HAPPY

Me Time

Write down the things that make you happy. Then, check the box every
day that you spend time with that activity.

	☐	☐	☐	☐	☐	☐	☐
	☐	☐	☐	☐	☐	☐	☐
	☐	☐	☐	☐	☐	☐	☐
	☐	☐	☐	☐	☐	☐	☐
	☐	☐	☐	☐	☐	☐	☐
	☐	☐	☐	☐	☐	☐	☐
	☐	☐	☐	☐	☐	☐	☐
	☐	☐	☐	☐	☐	☐	☐

NOTES:

Self Care

DAILY **INSPIRATION**

WATER INTAKE:

FITNESS **GOALS**

_____

_____

_____

One day at a time...

THANKFUL **FOR**

DAILY **MEALS**

BREAKFAST:

_____

_____

_____

LUNCH:

_____

_____

DINNER:

_____

_____

_____

SNACKS:

_____

_____

_____

_____

_____

Personal Goals

MY SELF GOALS FOR THIS YEAR:

2 THINGS I CAN CHANGE TO MEET MY GOALS:

MY GREATEST OBSTACLE GOING FORWARD:

Good things take time

Mental Health Monitor

DAILY

_____

_____

_____

_____

_____

_____

_____

_____

_____

_____

_____

_____

WEEKLY

_____

_____

_____

_____

_____

_____

_____

_____

_____

_____

_____

_____

PERSONAL REFLECTIONS

Self Care Goals

TIME FRAME	MY GOALS	STEPS I'LL TAKE

be wild ~ be true ~ be happy

Self Care Techniques

MIND

_____
_____
_____
_____
_____
_____
_____
_____
_____
_____
_____
_____

BODY

_____
_____
_____
_____
_____
_____
_____
_____
_____
_____
_____
_____

PERSONAL REFLECTIONS

One Day at a Time

		NOVEMBER				
S	M	T	W	T	F	S
					1	2
3	4	5	6	7	8	9
10	11	12	13	14	15	16
17	18	19	20	21	22	23
24	25	26	27	28	29	30

NOTES & REMINDERS

Positive Thinking

SELF CARE TO DO LIST:

- [ ] _____
- [ ] _____
- [ ] _____
- [ ] _____
- [ ] _____
- [ ] _____
- [ ] _____
- [ ] _____
- [ ] _____
- [ ] _____
- [ ] _____
- [ ] _____
- [ ] _____
- [ ] _____

PHYSICAL NEEDS

EMOTIONAL NEEDS

HOW I FEEL TODAY

I WANT TO WORK ON...

Self Care Checklist

GOALS	M	T	W	T	F	S	S
Got enough rest	○	○	○	○	○	○	○
Spent time outdoors	○	○	○	○	○	○	○
Drank enough water	○	○	○	○	○	○	○
Spent time doing Something that makes me happy.	○	○	○	○	○	○	○
Went for a walk or exercised.	○	○	○	○	○	○	○
Spent time with family	○	○	○	○	○	○	○
Meditated	○	○	○	○	○	○	○
Connected with friends	○	○	○	○	○	○	○
_____	○	○	○	○	○	○	○
_____	○	○	○	○	○	○	○
_____	○	○	○	○	○	○	○

NOTES:

Mood Meter

MONDAY
TUESDAY
WEDNESDAY
THURSDAY
FRIDAY
SATURDAY
SUNDAY

AM | PM

TRACK YOUR MOODS

COLOR SCALE

Grateful Thoughts

THIS WEEK I AM GRATEFUL FOR

I AM BLESSED TO HAVE THESE PEOPLE IN MY LIFE

5 REASONS TO BE THANKFUL

1
2
3
4
5

Self Care Log

HOW I CAN **MINIMIZE THE NEGATIVITY** IN MY LIFE

POSITIVE STEPS I CAN TAKE TO BE HAPPY

It Always Seems Impossible Until It's Done

Me Time

Write down the things that make you happy. Then, check the box every day that you spend time with that activity.

	☐ ☐ ☐ ☐ ☐ ☐ ☐
	☐ ☐ ☐ ☐ ☐ ☐ ☐
	☐ ☐ ☐ ☐ ☐ ☐ ☐
	☐ ☐ ☐ ☐ ☐ ☐ ☐
	☐ ☐ ☐ ☐ ☐ ☐ ☐
	☐ ☐ ☐ ☐ ☐ ☐ ☐
	☐ ☐ ☐ ☐ ☐ ☐ ☐
	☐ ☐ ☐ ☐ ☐ ☐ ☐

NOTES:

Self Care

DAILY **INSPIRATION**

WATER INTAKE:

FITNESS **GOALS**

_____

_____

_____

One day at a time...

THANKFUL **FOR**

DAILY **MEALS**

BREAKFAST:

_____

_____

_____

LUNCH:

_____

_____

_____

DINNER:

_____

_____

_____

SNACKS:

_____

_____

_____

_____

_____

Personal Goals

MY SELF GOALS FOR THIS YEAR:

2 THINGS I CAN CHANGE TO MEET MY GOALS:

MY GREATEST OBSTACLE GOING FORWARD:

Good things take time

Mental Health Monitor

DAILY

_____
_____
_____
_____
_____
_____
_____
_____
_____
_____
_____

WEEKLY

_____
_____
_____
_____
_____
_____
_____
_____
_____
_____
_____

PERSONAL REFLECTIONS

Self Care Goals

TIME FRAME	MY GOALS	STEPS I'LL TAKE

be wild ～ be true ～ be happy

Self Care Techniques

MIND

_____
_____
_____
_____
_____
_____
_____
_____
_____
_____
_____

BODY

_____
_____
_____
_____
_____
_____
_____
_____
_____
_____
_____

PERSONAL REFLECTIONS

One Day at a Time

DECEMBER

S	M	T	W	T	F	S
1	2	3	4	5	6	7
8	9	10	11	12	13	14
15	16	17	18	19	20	21
22	23	24	25	26	27	28
29	30	31				

NOTES & REMINDERS

Positive Thinking

SELF CARE TO DO LIST:

- [ ] _____
- [ ] _____
- [ ] _____
- [ ] _____
- [ ] _____
- [ ] _____
- [ ] _____
- [ ] _____
- [ ] _____
- [ ] _____
- [ ] _____
- [ ] _____
- [ ] _____
- [ ] _____

PHYSICAL NEEDS

EMOTIONAL NEEDS

HOW I FEEL TODAY

I WANT TO WORK ON...

Self Care Checklist

GOALS	M	T	W	T	F	S	S
Got enough rest	○	○	○	○	○	○	○
Spent time outdoors	○	○	○	○	○	○	○
Drank enough water	○	○	○	○	○	○	○
Spent time doing Something that makes me happy.	○	○	○	○	○	○	○
Went for a walk or exercised.	○	○	○	○	○	○	○
Spent time with family	○	○	○	○	○	○	○
Meditated	○	○	○	○	○	○	○
Connected with friends	○	○	○	○	○	○	○
_____	○	○	○	○	○	○	○
_____	○	○	○	○	○	○	○
_____	○	○	○	○	○	○	○

NOTES:

Mood Meter

MONDAY

TUESDAY

WEDNESDAY

THURSDAY

FRIDAY

SATURDAY

SUNDAY

AM | PM

TRACK YOUR MOODS

COLOR SCALE

Grateful Thoughts

THIS WEEK I AM GRATEFUL FOR

I AM BLESSED TO HAVE THESE PEOPLE IN MY LIFE

5 REASONS TO BE THANKFUL

1
2
3
4
5

Me Time

Write down the things that make you happy. Then, check the box every day that you spend time with that activity.

	☐ ☐ ☐ ☐ ☐ ☐ ☐
	☐ ☐ ☐ ☐ ☐ ☐ ☐
	☐ ☐ ☐ ☐ ☐ ☐ ☐
	☐ ☐ ☐ ☐ ☐ ☐ ☐
	☐ ☐ ☐ ☐ ☐ ☐ ☐
	☐ ☐ ☐ ☐ ☐ ☐ ☐
	☐ ☐ ☐ ☐ ☐ ☐ ☐
	☐ ☐ ☐ ☐ ☐ ☐ ☐

NOTES:

Self Care

DAILY **INSPIRATION**

WATER INTAKE:

FITNESS **GOALS**

_____
_____
_____

One day at a time…

THANKFUL **FOR**

DAILY **MEALS**

BREAKFAST:

_____
_____
_____

LUNCH:

_____
_____

DINNER:

_____
_____
_____

SNACKS:

_____
_____
_____
_____

Personal Goals

MY SELF GOALS FOR THIS YEAR:

2 THINGS I CAN CHANGE TO MEET MY GOALS:

MY GREATEST OBSTACLE GOING FORWARD:

Good things take time

Mental Health Monitor

DAILY

_____
_____
_____
_____
_____
_____
_____
_____
_____
_____
_____

WEEKLY

_____
_____
_____
_____
_____
_____
_____
_____
_____
_____
_____

PERSONAL REFLECTIONS

Made in the USA
Monee, IL
19 November 2019